WAN2TLK?

ltle bk
of txt
ms

WAN2HELP?

We are constantly updating
our files of text messages and
emoticons for the next edition of
this book. If you would like to add
variations of your own please
e-mail us at
jokes@michaelomarabooks.com

We will let you know if your
additions are going to be included.
Thank you

WAN2TLK?

ltle bk
of txt
msgs

First published in Great Britain in 2000 by
Michael O'Mara Books Limited
9 Lion Yard
Tremadoc Road
London SW4 7NQ

Copyright © 2000 by Michael O'Mara Books Limited

A CIP catalogue record for this book is available from the British Library

ISBN 1-85479-678-X

    12 13 14 15 16 17 18 19 20

Devised and edited by Gabrielle Mander

Cover Design: Design 23
Telephone supplied and used by kind permission of Motorola.

Designed and typeset by Design 23

www.mombooks.com

Made and printed in Great Britain by William Clowes, Beccles, Suffolk

CONTENTS

INTRODUCTION

Text messaging is the smart way to communicate in the 21st Century. Everyone, men and women, young and old use it, but especially the young, and it has become the fastest growing service on every network. Why?

Perhaps it is because it's discreet. You can set your phone to vibrate rather than ring when you receive a message and you don't cause a nuisance to others when you reply! We don't recommend it of course, but I understand from teachers that it has replaced passing notes in class as a way of expressing those irresistible asides or making plans for after school. It's cheaper than calling, so you don't use up precious call time as quickly – a boon to 'pay as you go' users especially. It is an international service, so that you can communicate when you are abroad without having to buy extra cards or adaptations for your phone and all at local rates.

All very sensible reasons to join the communication revolution. But if you are still unconvinced, you might like to know that it is also great fun. You can learn and contribute to a whole new language, created by the users. Surveys show that men find it especially tempting to express their feelings by text messaging, especially those tricky ones like 'I love you' and 'I'm sorry!' Young people use it to finalize their infinitely flexible plans and text messaging is a great way to introduce yourself to a stranger at a noisy club or party. Members of the Muslim community in the UK have even used it to call the faithful to prayer. Text messaging has its own grammar and 'netiquette' developed from e-mail and Internet chat rooms, so don't use capital letters – it is classed as shouting and considered very rude!

WAN2TLK? contains all the information you need to start chatting, with over 1000 abbreviations and 'emoticons' and their meanings. So just go to the messages option 'write messages' on your phone and start to type. It will guess what you are trying to say, or you can press the options menu and insert words, numbers or symbols – then send. This little phrase book will make you an expert in no time and you can use it for Internet communication too. Welcome to their world.

WAN2TLK?
Basic emoticons

Chatting to old friends and making new ones on your mobile 'phone, or on the internet can be the best and cheapest way to make plans, have a row, start a romance or end an affair and it's discreet! But your messages can be open to misinterpretation when the person you are talking to can't see you or hear the inflection in your voice. The mood of your message is one of the hardest things to convey 'Emoticons' are a shorthand way of explaining or elaborating on your meaning. Made from punctuation marks on your keypad, they take up very little space, can be keyed in seconds and may make the difference between a lasting friendship and social disaster.

The basic smiley face is just a colon, a dash and a close bracket **:-)** and yet when you rotate it through 90˚ it becomes a smile. Most emoticons rotate through 90˚ although some are front facing. The sub-text of your words, acronyms or abbreviations will become crystal clear to anyone reading them if you punctuate your message with emoticons, whenever and wherever you feel like it. Emoticons can also be used just for fun, and a lot of creativity goes into making pictures and jokes using the minimum number of characters. The examples below are the basic emoticons in use. You will find even shorter versions, jokes and pictures as well as acronyms and abbreviations in the pages that follow.   **HAND :-) !!**

Emoticon	Meaning
;-) ;) ;->	winking happy faces; for comments said tongue-in-cheek
:-(:(:-<	sad, disappointed faces
:-p :-P	faces with tongues stuck out at you
:-]	I am very jolly
:-[	I am down and unhappy
:-D	I am very happy
:-I	I couldn't care less
8-) 8) B-) B)	smiling faces from someone who wears glasses or sun glasses, or has a wide-eyed look

>:-)	a devil with a grin; for those devilish remarks
O:-)	an angel with a halo; for those innocent remarks.
<:-)	wearing a dunce's cap; for those stupid questions.
m(_ _)m	deep bow used for apologizing or expressing thanks (viewed from the front).
*^_^*	a huge dazzling grin
:-)	I'm joking
;-)	I have just made a flirtatious and/or sarcastic remark "don't hit me for what I just said"

:-(	I did not like that last statement or I am upset or depressed about something
:->	I have just made a really biting sarcastic remark
>:->	I have just made a really devilish remark
>;->	I have just made a very lewd remark
:-	I am confused/undecided/doubtful
:-Q	I have no idea what you are talking about
:-S	words fail me
:-@	I am shocked/screaming

:-O	I am surprised/ yelling or ("uh oh!")
:->>	a huge smile
I-(I-)	I am very tired
-text	Underline text
TEXT	YELLING

WAN2TLKFST?
Abbreviations and acronyms for fast talkers

AAM	as a matter of fact
AB	ah bless!
AFAIC	as far as I'm concerned
AFAIK	as far as I know
AKA	also known as
ASAP	as soon as possible
ATB	all the best
B	be
BCNU	be seeing you

Bwd	backward
B4	before
BBFN	bye bye for now
BFN	bye for now
BRB	be right back
BTW	by the way
BYKT	but you knew that
C	see
CMIIW	correct me if I'm wrong
CU	see you
CYA	see you

CUL8R	see you later
CW2CU	can't wait to see you
Doin	doing
EOL	end of lecture
FAQ	frequently asked question(s)
FITB	fill in the blank
F2T	free to talk
FOAD	f'off and die
FUBAR	f'd up beyond all recognition
Fwd	forward
FWIW	for what it's worth

FYI	for your information
Gonna	going to
Gr8	great
GD&R	grinning, ducking and running (after snide remark)
GG	good game
HAND	have a nice day
H8	hate
HTH	hope this/to help(s)
Hot4U	hot for you
IAC	in any case
IAE	in any event

IANAL	I am not a lawyer (but...)
ICCL	I couldn't care less
ICL	in Christian love
IDK	I don't know
IYSS	if you say so
IHTFP	I have truly found paradise (or: I hate this f'n place)
IIRC	if I recall correctly
ILUVU	I love you
ILUVUMED	I love you more each day
IMCO	in my considered opinion
IMHO	in my humble opinion

IMNSHO	in my not so humble opinion
IMO	in my opinion
IOW	in other words
ITYFIR	I think you'll find I'm right
IUTLUVUBIAON	I used to love you but it's all over now
IYDKIDKWD	if you don't know I don't know who does
IYKWIM	if you know what I mean
IYKWIMAITYD	if you know what I mean and I think you do
JM2p	just my 2 pennyworth
KIT	keep in touch

L8	late
L8r	later
Luv	love
LOL	lots of luck or laughing out loud
MGB	may God bless
MHOTY	my hat's off to you
MMD	make my day
MMDP	make my day punk!
Mob	mobile
Msg	message
MYOB	mind your own business

NE	any
NE1	anyone
NH	nice hand
NO1	no one
NRN	no reply necessary
OIC	oh, I see
OTOH	on the other hand
PCM	please call me
PITA	pain in the ass
PLS	please
PPL	people

PS	post script
R	are
ROF	rolling on the floor
ROFL	rolling on the floor laughing
ROTFL	rolling on the floor laughing
RSN	really soon now
RU	are you?
RUOK?	are you OK?
SITD	still in the dark
SIT	stay in touch
SMS	short message service

SOHF	sense of humour failure
SOME1	someone
Stra	stray
SWG	scientific wild guess
SWALK	sealed with a loving kiss
THNQ	thank you
Thx	thanks
TIA	thanks in advance
TIC	tongue in cheek
Ti2GO	time to go
TPTB	the powers that be

TTFN	ta ta for now
TTUL	talk to you later
TWIMC	to whom it may concern
TUVM	thank you very much
U	you
UR	you are
WAN2	want to
WAN2TLK?	want to talk?
W/	with
Wknd	weekend
WRT	with respect to

WTTW	word to the wise
WUCIWUG	what you see is what you get
X	kiss
Xoxoxoxo	hugs and kisses
YKWYCD	you know what you can do
YMMV	your mileage may vary (you may not have the same luck I did)
YR	your
YTLKIN2ME?	you talking to me?
YWIA	you're welcome in advance
YYSSW	yeah, yeah, sure, sure, whatever

1	one
2	to, too
2day	today
2moro	tomorrow
2nite	tonight
3sum	threesome
4	for
<G	grinning
<J>	joking
<L>	laughing
<O>	shouting
<S>	smiling
<Y>	yawning

YYSSW
Yeah, Yeah, Sure, Sure, Whatever!
Tell me how you really feel

:-)	ha ha
I-)	hee hee
I-D	ho ho
:->	hey hey
:-(	boo hoo
:-I	hmmm
:-O	oops
:-*	ooops
:-o	uh oh!

{}	'no comment'
I:-O	no explanation given
:-o	oh, no!
#:-o	oh, no!
:-0	ohhhhhh!
I:-O	big ohhhhhh!
<:-O	eeek!
O:-)	for those innocent souls
%+{	from the loser of a fight
<:-)	for dumb questions
:-)))	reeeaaaalllly happy
;-) or P-)	wink, wink, nudge, nudge

:-P	nyahhhh!
:-7	that was a wry remark
*8=(:	I am a blithering idiot
>;-('	I am spitting mad
:-)~	I am drooling (in anticipation)
:-9	I am licking my lips.
(-:	I am left-handed
:'-(	I am crying
<3	I love you
:'-)	I am so happy, I am crying
:~~(	I am bawling

:-@	I am screaming
:-&	I feel tongue tied.
:*(@)	I am drunk and shouting
<&-I	I feel foolish and tearful
((H)))	a big hug
:-X	a big wet kiss
(:-D	I can't keep a secret or you are a blabber mouth
:-S	my last message didn't make sense
:-D	I am laughing (at you!)
I-O	I am bored/yawning/snoring.

:-o zz z z Z Z	I am bored
:^U	I turn my face away
:^Y	I turn my poker face away
:-X	my lips are sealed
:-#	my lips are still sealed
:-C	I am really bummed
:-/	I am sceptical
:-T	I am keeping a straight face
o'!	I am feeling pretty grim (profile)
o'"	I am pursing my lips (profile)
o'J	smiling (profile)

o'P	sticking tongue out (profile)
o'r	sticking tongue out (profile)
o'T	keeping a straight face (profile)
o'U	yawning (profile)
o'V	shouting (profile)
o'Y	whistling (profile)
o'\	frowning (profile)
o'v	talking (profile)
o'w	lying(profile)
7=^>	I am happy (3/4 view)
:-S	I am confused
:*(	I am crying softly

:-@!	I am cursing
:-"	whistling casually
:-e	I am disappointed
(:-...	I am heart-broken
:-t	I am cross and pouting
I-I	I am going to sleep
:*)	I am drunk
%-)	I am drunk but happy
L	I am blotto (sideways)
:*)?	are you drunk?
:#)	I am drunk every night

%*@:-(	I am hungover with a headache
%-<l>	I am drunk with laughter
:-W	I am lying (forked tongue)
:^)	I have personality
d :-)	hats off to your great idea
:-(*)	that comment made me sick
(><)	I am anally retentive
(@ @)	You're kidding!
(:-lK-	this is a formal message
(-_-)	this is my secret smile
@*&$!%	you know what that means...

(O—<	I suspect something fishy is going on
-/-	I am stirring up trouble
**-(	I am very, very shocked
:^D	great! I like it!
M:-)	I salute you (respect)
:-$	put your money where your mouth is
:+(	I am hurt by that remark
:~(	I'm feeling put out
>-COD	I am "floundering" for something to say
/O\	I am ducking.

.^,	I am looking sideways/happy
:-L	I am blank with cigarette or pipe
=-o	I am surprised
<=-O	I am frightened
=-◇	I am awe struck
)I-[	I am tired and grumpy and very unhappy.
(]:-)	I am gung ho
$->	I am happily excited
I-o	I am squinting while talking
:~(~~~	I am moved to tears
O-(==<	I am chastised and/or chagrined

`__.`	I am properly chastised and/or chagrined
`__/~-'~\_/`	I don't follow your line of thought
`I-{`	"Good Grief!" (Charlie Brown?)
`===:[OO']>:===`	I have been railroaded
`=^)`	I am open minded
`\o/`	PTL (praise the lord, or pass the loot?) (sideways)
`B-D`	"Serves you right, dummy!!"
`>w`	oh really! (ironic)
`8-]`	"wow, maaan"
`OO`	Please read now (headlights on msg)

O-G-<	me, me, me (pointing to self (midget whole body)
O-S-<	I am in a hurry (midget whole body)
O-Z-<	in a big hurry (midget whole body)

WUCIWUG?

What you see is what you get
So what do you look like really?

]-I	I am wearing sunglasses
B:-)	I am wearing sunglasses on my head (cool)
B-I	I am wearing cheap sunglasses
::-)	I am wearing normal glasses
g-)	I am wearing pince-nez glasses
V^J	with glasses, seen from the left side (portrait, talking)
(-E:	I am wearing bifocals
B-)	I am wearing horn-rimmed glasses

R-)	I am wearing broken glasses
I-(	I have lost my contact lenses
@:-)	I am wearing a turban.
:-)8	I am well dressed
:-)-8	I am a big girl
B*)	I have a moustache and designer sunglasses!
:-()	I have a moustache
:-3	I have a handlebar moustache
:-=)	I am an older man/woman with a moustache
:-#l	I have a bushy moustache

(:-{~	I am bearded
:-)##	I am seriously bearded
:-)}	I have a goatee beard
:^{)>	I have a moustache and a beard
(8-{)}	I am bearded with a moustache and glasses
I:-)	I have a monobrow
/;-)	I have a cockeyed monobrow
`:-)	I shaved one of my eyebrows off this morning.
,.'v	I have short hair (profile)
,o'v	I have short hair (profile)
=o'v	I have a mohawk (profile)

~o'v	I have a long fringe (profile)
?:-)	I have wavy hair, parted on right
}:-)	my hair is parted in the middle in an updraft
(-)	I need a haircut
@:-}	I am just back from the hairdresser
~:-P	I am thinking and steaming having only one single hair
{:-)	I am wearing a toupee
;:-)	I am wearing a really bad toupee
}:-(	my toupee is at risk form a high wind

42

r:-)	I have a ponytail
@:-)	I have wavy hair
#:-)	I have tangled hair
&:-)	I have curly hair
@.'v	I have curly hair (profile)
?:)	I have a single curl of hair
{:-{)}	I have a new hair style, moustache and beard
:-(>~	I just washed my goatee, and I can't do a thing with it.
/8^{~	I have a lopsided hair line, glasses, moustache, and goatee
&:-]	I am very handsome with square jaw

&8-]	I too am very handsome, also with square jaw
:-~)	I have a cold
:x(	I habe a code in by dose
:-R	I have the flu
:%)%	I have acne
:-))	I have a double chin
:-#	I wear braces
:-{#}	I am wearing braces too
H-)	I am cross-eyed
:^)	I have a broken nose
:v)	I have a broken nose, but the other way

`}:^#)`	I have a pointy nose
`o^v`	I have a pointy nose (profile)
`:=)`	I have two noses.
`?-(`	I have a black eye
`:<)`	I am a public school student
`I-I`	this is me asleep
`(-.-)Zzz...`	this is me sleeping (sideways)
`(,'%/)`	I have slept too long on one side
`#(,'%/)`	I have slept too long on one side and didn't have time to wash my hair
`*<8-)X`	I am wearing a party outfit with hat and bow-tie

(}-8]	I am left-handed and bearded with glasses and headphones
do'v	I am wearing a hard hat (profile)
(:-)}	I am bald and bearded
:-{}	I am wearing lipstick
:-+	I may be wearing too much lipstick
:-) ,	I have an outie belly button
:-) .	I have an innie belly button

GET REAL! VITAL INFO

:-Q	I smoke
:-"	I am a heavy smoker
:/i	no smoking
(^^)y-~~~	I am smoking now (sideways)
:-j	I am smoking and smiling
:Ui	I am smoking as we speak
:Uj	I am smoking and smiling as we speak
:-?	I smoke a pipe
:-`	I am spitting out my chewing tobacco.

:-[	I am a vampire
:-E	I am a bucktoothed vampire
+-:-)	I am the Pope (or other religious leader)
-:-)	I am a punk rocker
-:-(	real punk rockers don't smile
:-) ... :-(... :-) ... :-(	I am a manic depressive
O-)	I am a scuba diver
:%)	I am an accountant
:?)	I am a philosopher
L:-)	I have just graduated
C:-)	I am modest with a large brain capacity

&;-P	I am a suave guy on the make.
{{-}}}	I'm a refugee from the '60's
(:-) ?	I am having a sex change
*:-} 8 8-	I am a transvestite
:-) : 8-^-	I need some corrective surgery
:-\ : 8o	I have just had a cold shower
:-)K-	I am wearing a shirt and tie
={:-)]	the answer wasn't in the bottle
*8-I	I am a nerd
!8-)	I am a nerd with combed hair
*X-I	I am a dead nerd

:-)I	I'm going out on the town
~:o	I am a baby
~:@	I am a baby with a dummy
>[:^)	I watch too much TV
!#!^*&~ >:-(	I am very angry after losing hours of work
+<#^v	I am your knight in shining armour (profile)
#!^~/	I am kissing and wearing shades (profile)
*<o'v	I am wearing a bobble cap (profile)
I:/	I am constipated

O :-)	I am an angel (at heart, at least)
<I-)	I am Chinese
<I-(	I am Chinese and I don't like these kind of jokes
:-)*	I speak Esperanto
C=:-)	I am a chef
***<:-)**	I am wearing a Santa Claus hat
3:]	I have a pet like this
3:[	my pet is vicious
E-:-)	I am a ham radio operator
%-6	I am braindead.

`[:-)`	I am wearing a walkman
`d:-)`	I am wearing a baseball cap
`q:-)`	I am wearing a baseball cap backwards
`(:I`	I am an egghead
`<:-I`	I am a dunce
`:-0`	I'm not deaf (Quiet please)
`.-)`	I have only one eye
`,-)`	ditto...but I'm winking
`X-(`	I have just died
`8 :-)`	I am a wizard
`:-)^<`	I am a big boy

:-)8<	I am a big girl
:-]	I am a blockhead
:-}X	I wear a bow-tie
!#!^*&:-)	I am schizophrenic
<l==l)	I have a car
.—-...	I am an AB Ǝ A fan

MDGTMSGES
Even shorter short hand

A lot of these can be typed without noses to make midget messages for really fast communication.

:)	happy
:]	friendly
=)	friendly 2
:}	what?
:>	what?
:@	what?
:C	what?

:Q	what?
:D	laughter
:) :) :)	loud guffaw
:I	hmmm...
;)	smirking
:(	sad
:[	real downer
; (	chin up
:O	yelling.
:V	shouting
:c	really unhappy

:C	unbelieving
:/)	not funny
:?	licking lips
:~)	yummee
:8	talking out both sides of your mouth
:,(	crying
:Y	a quiet aside
;?	wry remark, tongue in cheek
;}	leer
:I :-	deja' vu
::=))	double vision

[!]	hug
[]	hugs and ...
:*	kisses
I*	kiss (eyes closed)
:-	male
>	female
: t	pouting
II	asleep
^o	snoring
&I	that made me cry
:k	biting my lip

:]	biting sarcasm
:-q	trying to touch tongue to nose
'!	(profile) grim
""	(profile) pursing lips
'J	(profile) smiling
'P	(profile) sticking tongue out
'T	(profile) keeping a straight face
'U	(profile) yawning
'V	(profile) shouting
'Y	(profile) whistling
'	(profile) frowning

oo-	puzzled, confused
'r	(profile) sticking tongue out
'v	(profile) talking
'w	(profile) speaking with forked tongue
:")	embarrassed
__!	enough for now
:!	foot in mouth
8O	omigod!
:@	it's true, I swear
X-(	mad
>:-<	mad

&I	makes me cry
:(*)	makes me sick
:-S	makes no sense
o/	excuse me, not waving but drowning
IP	yuk
8	infinity
:-8(	condescending stare
8-I	suspense
^^	happiness (Japanese symbol)
^^;	embarrassment (Japanese symbol)

;;	sadness (Japanese symbol)
||*)	handshake accepted (taking)
M-),:X),:-M	sees no evil, hears no evil, speaks no evil
8-S	sees all evil
O+	for women's messages
^L^	happy (sideways)
^(^	happy variation (sideways)
^)^ ^(^	two people talking (sideways)
i-=<*i**	CAUTION: has flame thrower
i-=<* __.**	CAUTION: has flame thrower and uses it!

i-=<****** o-(==<	CAUTION: has flame thrower and uses it!
o=	a burning candle for flames (shouting messages of an unpleasant nature)
-=	a doused candle to end a flame
...—-...	S.O.S.
O>-◁=	messages of interest to women
O-&-<	I'm doing nothing (has arms crossed) (mini whole body)
:—————)	you are a big liar

WAN2CAPIC?
Want to see a picture?

@>—;—	rose
O:-)	angel
0*-)	angel winking
:= l	baboon
`AR~	baby elephant (sideways)
(:=	beaver
pq`#'	bull (sideways)
=:)	bunny
=:x	another bunny
}l{	butterfly

})i({	butterfly – an even prettier one
~M`'~	camel (sideways)
}:-X	cat
`'	cat's eyes in the night
__/\o_	caterpillar
8^	chicken
3:-o	cow
pp#	cow (sideways)
:3-]	dog
]B=8}	dragon
.V	duck

`(:<>`	another duck
`#B<>`	duck, with a spike haircut & Ray-Bans, quacking.
`6V)`	elephant
`<:3`	ferret
`>-^);>`	fish
`><FISH>`	fish
`>-",",",",-)D>`	fish
`9)`	frog
`>^,,^`	kitty cat
`@(*0*)@`	koala bear
`<:3 )~~~~`	mouse

~\\ (^o^) /~/~	octopus (Japanese symbol)
:=)	orangutan
:8)	pig
3:[	pitbull
~~8}	snake
∧o∧	spider
<:>==	turkey
(	unhappy Cheshire cat
'~;E	unspecified 4-legged creature
:<=	walrus
:V	woodpecker

WAN2CMORE?

_:^)	American Indian
>>>>>:=========	(asparagus)
C=:-)	chef
~:	child
*<<<<=	Christmas tree.
*<):o)	clown
*-=I8-D	clown
*(H	downhill skier
((Y))	fat lady
(((Y)))	fatter lady
(..(Y)..)	fattest lady

:))))	fat man
C:#	football player
/:-)	Frenchman with a beret
(D:-]	general
-(:-)	German soldier from WWI
oO:)&	grandmother
>:^(	headhunter (Amazon style)
I^o	hepcat
]:)I—<	king
+<II-)	knight
'v	knight (profile)
\.^./	lotus position, seen from above

{:-) 8 > <	mermaid.
^v^v^	mountains
/_/\	mountain range.
):-(	Nordic
P-(	pirate
Ic:()	pygmy with bone in hair
8x	scissors
*I:^)(.)(...)	snowman
>[I	television
#:o\:o/:o\:o/:oII	totem pole
-=#:-)	wizard
<*(:-?	a wizard who doesn't know the answer

WAN2SPTA*?
Famous for 15 seconds

: =)	Adolf Hitler
{:^=(	Adolf Hitler
{	Alfred Hitchcock
:-)==	Arnold Schwarzenegger
#:o+=	Betty Boop
&:-o-8-<	Betty Boop
:'O	Bob Hope
>8o!...	Bugs Bunny with carrot
IIII8^)X	Cat in the Hat

((: =)X	Charlie Chaplin
Cl:-=	Charlie Chaplin
:/7)	Cyrano de Bergerac
{:◇	Daffy Duck
C8<]	Darth Vader
(8=X	Death (Mr. Death to you) (skull & X bones)
:-8p	Dizzy Gillespie (puffed cheeks and trumpet)
:-) 8	Dolly Parton
:$)	Donald Trump
5:-)	Elvis

@:)	Elvis
EK(	Frankenstein
[:=I]	Frankenstein's monster
`,`,`,`,`:I	Mrs. Frankenstein's monster
:^{=	Frank Zappa
7:-)	Fred Flintstone
>>-O->	General Custer
I:['	Groucho Marx
(:^(	Jack Nicholson in Chinatown
?:^[]	Jim Carrey
:(=)	Jimmy Carter

:###)	Jimmy Durante
(8 {	John Lennon
:-.)	Madonna, Marilyn Monroe
8(:-)	Mickey Mouse
/V:/\	The Mummy
(Z(:^P	Napoleon
:—-)	Pinocchio
:'}	Richard Nixon
3:*>	Rudolph the reindeer
*<|:-)	Santa Claus
)-:|<*	Sanity Clause
:-) :-) :-) :-)	Shirley MacLaine

3 :-)	Bart Simpson
{8->	Bart Simpson
(_8^(I)	Homer Simpson
(_8(I)	Homer Simpson
@@@@:-)	Marge Simpson
{8-*	Maggie Simpson
{8-)	Lisa Simpson
B-(8	Sir Robin Day
:_(	Van Gogh
...(	Wile E. Coyote after attempt on road runner's life
=IB-{I###	ZZ Top

WAN2PLA?
**Do you want to play? –
Far fetched and fantasy**

:—-(Message about/from
                    someone sad because he or
                    she has a large nose

:-D*   I am laughing so hard that I
                    did not notice that a 5-legged
                    spider is hanging from my lip

>8-O-(&)   Message about/from
                    someone who has just
                    realized that they have a
                    tapeworm

~oE]:-l   Fisherperson heading for
                    market with a basket on his
                    or her head containing a
                    three-legged octopus that is
                    giving off smell rays

>:-[-{9	Person who is none too pleased to be giving birth to a squirrel
}:^#})	I am happy though my toupee is being blown upwards and I have a bushy moustache, a pointy nose and a double chin
+-(	I have been shot between the eyes
(XOII)	Double hamburger with lettuce and tomato please
(: (=I	Message about/from someone wearing a ghost costume (mini whole body)
(-o-)	Imperial Tie Fighter ("Star Wars")
;-)}</////>	Corporate-type guy

&B-]}</////>	A corporate-type with aviator glasses, wavy hair & tie.
:-)-O	Smiling doctor with stethoscope
*;~i	A lady replying to a guy by closing both eyes & puffing nonchalantly on her cigarette
(:><	A thief: hands up! (mini whole body)
:-) >=>	Message about/from someone reading a book
>]}	Message about/from a dragon wearing sunglasses
{:-l 8( )>	You are going to be a father!

>:-(8 >	Message about/from a female after reading sexist opinions on feminists
@O=E<=	Message about/from a woman in a skirt wearing a turtleneck sweater (mini whole body)
B-)-[<	Message about/from a man wearing sunglasses and swimming trunks (mini whole body)
o>8<l=	Messages about/to interesting women (mini whole body)
:-)<////>	Message from/about a guy with a bad tie on
<\\\\\>(-:	Message from/about a left-handed guy with a bad tie on

::-bld-::	Message about/from a person wearing glasses and sticking out tongue at mirror
:-) (-: + :-o o-: + :-Pd-:	a kissing (sequence)
@@B-)	Message about/from a bouffant woman with catseye frame glasses
<<<<(:-)	Message from a hat salesman
<&&>	Message concerning rubber chickens
>< ><	Message about/to someone wearing argyle socks
<{:-}>	Message in a bottle
<:-)<<l	Message from a space rocket

?-(	Message about someone with a black eye
:	Message about fuzzy things
*:**	Message about fuzzy things with fuzzy moustaches
%-)	Message about people with broken glasses
(:-)	Messages dealing with bicycle helmets
(:-$	Message indicating person is ill-informed about the Renaissance
<@:{(>X	Message about/from a moustached Chinese man with a toupee, goatee and bow tie

2BI^2B	Message about Shakespeare
OO	A guy is mooning you
O:O	A girl is mooning you
:-))-:	Masking theatrical comments
C=>8*)	Message about/from devilish chef with glasses and a moustache
C=}>;*{(O)	Message about/from a drunk, devilish chef with a toupee in an updraft, a moustache, and a double chin
}:~#})	Message about/ from a bushy-moustached ugly-nosed man or woman with a double-chin

I-Q	Message about/from a Chinese person smoking and yelling
-:	Message about/from someone upside down with a brick in his mouth
@&o/	Message about/from a tearful-sceptic, wearing a turban
{l^x~	Message about/ from someone with hair-parted-in-the-middle, kissing and drooling
<X	Message about/from someone crazy and giving a wet kiss
+-::(@)	Message about/from a religious wearing normal glasses but shouting

<,-?	Message about/from someone with one-winking-eye-only and smoking a pipe
<&*c	Message about/from someone tearful, drunk and unhappy
>&-r	Message about/from someone tearful and sticking tongue out
{:0	Message about/from orator wearing a toupee
}::-?	Message about/from someone wearing a toupee in a updraft, wearing normal glasses and smoking a pipe
B:*/	Message about/from someone drunk and undecided with sunglasses on head

*^O	Message about/from a crazy-big-mouth
<:@0	Message about/from a pig-nosed orator
<8-~)	Message about/from a swimmer with a cold and smiling
>I*b	Message about/from a drunk pointing the tongue out
@0-(	Message about/from a sad scuba-diver wearing a turban
(B:o#	Message about/from an egg-head with sunglasses on head and wearing braces
(8*<	Message from/about an egg-head-swimmer, drunk and mad

*.-)	Message about/from someone one-eyed but smiling
~~0{	Message about/from a burning scuba-diver with a moustache
OOOOBc~	Marge Simpson, unhappy wearing glasses and drooling
OOOO:@[	pig-nosed -Marge Simpson- vampire
OOOO-{I	Marge Simpson-crazy person with a moustache
OOOOX-~(	dead-Marge Simpson-sad and with a cold
<:-@ 8-	Message about/from a male screaming
<:-) >–	Message about/from a female smiling

[B-~[	Message about/from a vampire wearing a walkman, glasses and with a cold
***!#^!*,-{**	Message about/from a schizophrenic, one-winking-eye-only and undecided with a moustache
***!#^!*lo#**	Message about/from a schizophrenic wearing braces
***!#^!*:@)**	Message about/from a pig-nosed, smiling schizophrenic
***!#^!*:@[**	Message about/from a pig-nosed schizophrenic vampire
***!#^!*loO**	Message about/from a schizophrenic-big-mouth user snoring

!#^!:-)	Message about/from a schizophrenic ,smiling
*(	Message about/from someone crazy and frowning
>8-<	Message about/from someone devilish, surprised and mad
::-{}	Message about/from someone wearing normal glasses and wearing lipstick
@::-x	Message about/from someone wearing a turban, normal glasses and kissing
@,^V	Message about/from someone with one-winking-eye-only, wearing a turban and shouting

<8-{D	Message about/from someone happy, wearing sunglasses and with a moustache
@8[	Message about/from a surprised vampire wearing a turban
<B:-/~	Message about/from someone undecided with sunglasses on head and drooling
[8*I	Message about/from someone drunk with a walkman and wearing sunglasses
@:-v	Message about/from someone wearing a turban and speaking
<B-~D	Message about/from someone happy, wearing glasses and with a cold

<8*p	Message about/from someone surprised-drunk pointing the tongue out
<8-{l	Message about/from a foolish swimmer with a moustache
*<:{	Message about/from someone with a moustache and wearing a Santa Claus hat
@:*&	Message about/from someone drunk, tongue-tied and wearing a turban
+-X-(	Message about/from someone dead, religious and frowning
@.-(@)	Message about/from someone with one-eye-only wearing a turban and shouting

@B-O~	Message about/from someone with a big-mouth wearing a turban, glasses and drooling
<B:^b	Message about/from someone with sunglasses on head and pointing the tongue out
<0-)	Message about/from a scuba-diver, smiling
{B-	Message about/from someone with hair-parted-in-the-middle, sceptical, with glasses
<8r	Message about/from someone wearing sunglasses and sticking tongue out
{loX	Message about/from someone with lips-sealed, wearing a toupee

`<8^)`	Message about/from a swimmer smiling
`87)`	cartoon character with a long nose and happy.
`~87(`	cartoon character unhappy that he has only one hair on his head
`%87)`	cartoon character happy he has his curly hair
`87D`	cartoon character with a long nose...and VERY happy
`87P O>w`	cartoon character enjoying eating his ice cream cone
``87P`` O>w``	cartoon character REALLY enjoying eating his ice cream cone

FULL ON

^_^	<	basic happy (Japanese style)
;_;	|	Crying (Japanese style)
@_@	<	Boggle eyed, or glasses (Japanese style)
(_o_)		kowtowing (bowing) person (Japanese style)
*^_^*		blushing (Japanese style)
^_^;;;		embarassed; cold sweat (Japanese style)
^^;;;		embarassed; cold sweat (Japanese style)
`\=o-o=/'		I am wearing glasses

())=(	I am drinking wine
-,-	I am sleepy
-.-	I am sleepy too
(o)(o)	I am a well-endowed female
>[]I	I am watching television
oo—-oo-Bo	I am a truck driver
,,,^..^,,,	I am being watched by a cat peeking over a fence
(^o^)	I am joyously singing
(^.^)/	waving hello (Japanese style)
(;.;)/~	waving goodbye (Japanese style)

(>_<)	I am furious
(=_=)~	I am sleepy (Japanese style)
(g_g)	I am sleepy
{{(>_<)}}	I am freezing (Japanese style)
(*_*)	I am in love
($_$)	I am being greedy
(x_x)	I may be dead
(u_u)	I am sleeping
(OvO)	I am a nightowl

(^-^)	another smile
<^O^>	I am laughing loudly
(@_@)	I am stunned
(o_o)	I am shocked

Now you can order other little books directly from
Michael O'Mara Books
All at £1.99 each including postage (UK only)

The Little Book of Farting ISBN 1-85479-445-0
The Little Book of Stupid Men ISBN 1-85479-454-X
The Little Toilet Book ISBN 1-85479-456-6
The Little Book of Pants 2 ISBN 1-85479-557-0
The Little Book of Revenge ISBN 1-85479-562-7
The Little Book of Voodoo ISBN 1-85479-560-0
The Little Book of Blondes ISBN 1-85479-558-9
The Little Book of Bums ISBN 1-85479-561-9
The Little Book of Magical Love Spells 1SBN 1-85479-559-7

Postage and Packing outside the UK:
Europe: add 20% of retail price,
rest of the world: add 30% of retail price

To order any Michael O'Mara Book
Please call our credit card order line 020 8324 5652